Drop Your Cape:
A Guide To Increase Self-Care, Wellness and Strength

Kiara Moore, MA, LPCMH

Table of Contents

Introduction

I'm so excited to share with you my personal mantra, which is "**drop the cape**." Let's release the Superwoman Syndrome, and let's learn to take care of ourselves through self-care, wellness and strength. You may be wondering, what is the *Superwoman Syndrome* (aka the cape)? I define Superwoman Syndrome/the cape as the thought or notion that you have to be everything for everyone, all the time. Women are strong, powerful, intelligent, thoughtful, nurturing, and we can do all things. However, we have mixed up the message that we *can* do all things with we *have* to do all things. This message reinforces our belief that we have to wear the cape. But we do not have to do all and be all for everyone. We have taken on the notion that we have to fix things, fix meals and fix people. However, that is not our job, nor is it our responsibility.

Most of us have seen our mothers and grandmothers exude strength, but we have also watched them neglect themselves on a personal level. Yes, sometimes we have to put on our cape, get into survival mode to get things done, and look fabulous while doing it! However, we have to remember that above all else, we are human; and if we end the day feeling broken, then we must not be paying attention to what our bodies are saying.

We have heard time and time again that we can't pour from an empty vessel, so it's important for us as women to build our own strength, and take care of ourselves before we even think about taking care of anyone else. We have to put our own well-being first. We also have to show the next generation how to live a healthier life by exemplifying self-care and healthy boundaries.

Self-Care

Self-care is not selfish.

SELF-CARE IS NOT SELFISH.

From this day forward, make your health, your wellness, and your life a priority. How many women have put aside their goals and dreams to help others? *There comes a point in life when we have to say we've done enough for others and we are going to do for ourselves.* In order to make yourself a priority, you have to drop the cape.

Some of our capes aren't easily removed and may need to be unstitched from the fibers of our being. We have to do the work to remove the deep-rooted ideals to save the world. We do not have to save the world! But we do have to save ourselves.

Life is short, and I guarantee you that the people who love you want you to be around for a long time. They would much rather have the healthier you and not the burned out, worried and stressed you. So, if we take the 8 areas of wellness (physical, emotional, spiritual, intellectual, financial, occupational, social

3

and environmental) and make them a priority in life, then we will achieve self-care. Now, self-care is not something that is one-and-done, and it is often misrepresented as spa days or a day off. Don't get me wrong; that's very much a part of self-care, but it's not the only part of self-care. Getting your nails, hair and makeup done or a new outfit will only give you a temporary boost in mood. When practicing self-care, you need to feel refreshed, renewed and revived. In addition to those activities, if we focus on the 8 areas of wellness, then we will have a deeper level of self-care, and that's what I want everyone to achieve. Let's retrain our brain to think of self-care as giving yourself the time, attention, nurture and care that we give to those around us.

Let's begin with evaluating your starting point.

On a scale of 1 to 10, with 1 being not at all and 10 being very much, rate how you feel right now in the following categories:

Satisfied with your current life
1 2 3 4 5 6 7 8 9 10

Fulfilled in your career
1 2 3 4 5 6 7 8 9 10

Satisfied with your current level of self-care
1 2 3 4 5 6 7 8 9 10

Fulfilled in your relationships
1 2 3 4 5 6 7 8 9 10

Feeling overwhelmed
1 2 3 4 5 6 7 8 9 10

Feeling anxious
1 2 3 4 5 6 7 8 9 10

Feeling restless
1 2 3 4 5 6 7 8 9 10

Feeling underappreciated or undervalued
1 2 3 4 5 6 7 8 9 10

In need of a break/vacation
1 2 3 4 5 6 7 8 9 10

In need of professional/personal boundaries
1 2 3 4 5 6 7 8 9 10

Reflection Questions

- Did any of your scores shock you?
- Were you satisfied with your ratings?
- If not, what can you do to improve that area of your life?
- How do you implement self-care in your life?
- What can you do to improve and prioritize your self-care?

The Cape

Why is it that we (yes, I'm including myself) are so readily able and willing to sacrifice ourselves for everyone else, and in situations that we most likely didn't create? Let's break down "the cape" a little further. On one hand, we are viewed as a strong, put together, get-it-done woman. On the other hand, some of the reasons we do so much is because of:

- Legacy of "the cape"
- Trauma response/abandonment
- Trust issues
- Believing you can do it faster and better than others
- Wanting to be independent
- Wanting all the credit
- Past disappointments
- Enabling instead of teaching
- Not wanting to let others down
- Thinking you can take the pressure better
- Pressure to perform
- Poor boundaries

Again, let's make it clear: *there are times when the cape/superpowers are necessary in our lives and careers.* If you have responsibilities, deadlines, sick children or a chaotic schedule, you have to wear your cape. If you are a single parent, entrepreneur, or working towards a goal, you have to wear your cape. In these moments and situations, wearing a cape is necessary to progress, accomplish your goal, and succeed. However, no superhero is constantly armed and ready for battle. They don't live in their cape. Once the battle is over, superheroes go home. When troubles arise, they gear up and go.

My goal for this guide is to show you the importance of taking your cape off and living your life. Put your cape on when it's necessary, but don't live with it on. Staying in survival mode, a constant state of anxiety, or an elevated mood will only break the body down. You don't want to go from full capacity to incapacitated because you focused more on your strength versus the rest of your human nature.

Legacy of the Cape

All of our early thoughts, opinions and behaviors are learned from those closest to us. Whether we want to accept it or not many of us are just like our parents. The only way to prevent this is to be intentional at not perpetuating the same mistakes. For most of us with the Superwoman Syndrome, it is likely that we had very strong and resilient women in our lives. These strong women showed us how to survive and show up every time. Unfortunately, they also showed us how to neglect ourselves for the good of the family and sacrifice it all. While they survived this way, we can express our resilience in ways that will have a healthier impact on our own lives and the generations coming after us.

Reflection Questions

Be honest with yourself.

- When did you first realize you were wearing the cape?
- What drives that force within you to operate at high intensity in superwoman mode?
- What memories do you have of the superwoman in your life?
- What did you learn from the superwoman in your life?

Trauma Response & Past Disappointments

When we experience tough or traumatic events, our bodies go into defense mode to protect us against future or similar pain. This response is a necessary survival skill. However, it's easy to become overprotective, and being too protective or defensive can have negative effects on your relationships and views. For example, if you grew up watching a parent struggle financially, you may have internalized that experience by saying you would never struggle in the same ways. So, you work tirelessly trying to prevent the same struggle or prevent any dependence on others. This defense or behavior pattern may also prevent you from asking for help when you really need it, causing you to ignore important signals from your body all because you don't want to experience those same feelings from your childhood.

While preventing those negative feelings appear to be a positive goal, what are you sacrificing? Rest? Companionship? Vulnerability? This is just one example, but Superwomen often carry a lot of defense mechanisms and wear a tough exterior to prevent hurt and pain.

Another example is avoiding vulnerability. Many experiences cause fear or avoidance of vulnerability due to the risk of getting hurt. While being hurt is a possibility, it is also possible that this fear/avoidance will result in a struggle to make genuine connections. Some people try avoiding vulnerability to prevent disappointment, being hurt, let down, or taken advantage of. This will also cause you to isolate and increase your rate of burnout, loneliness and isolation. Vulnerability allows you to be seen, heard and understood. If you are avoiding vulnerability by doing everything yourself, then you are preventing yourself from fully being seen or heard. While it appears to be a protective layer to keep you safe, the barriers against vulnerability also keep out the compassion, reciprocated love and connection you deserve.

Reflection Questions

- Has a negative experience shaped your life and how you respond to tasks, people and stress?
- Do you find this response effective? Does it allow you to make meaningful relationships that are equal in both giving and taking?

Cognitive Distortions

A cognitive distortion is a negative way of thinking about something. The thought, "Nobody likes me," is an example of a cognitive distortion. It overgeneralizes and discounts the many people that do like and even love you.

There are many other types of cognitive distortions: overgeneralizing, blaming, catastrophizing, magnifying, mind-reading, emotional reasoning and more. Usually, these thoughts are only based on your personal experience and from your perspective. Distortions are fed by irrational and exaggerated sub-thoughts. For Superwomen, the driving forces for our behavioral patterns are the result of our cognitive distortions. This goes back to those false thoughts listed earlier:

- I have to.
- I can do it all.
- I can do it better and faster.
- I can take the pressure better.
- I want to be independent.
- I want all the credit.
- I don't want to let others down.

In order to challenge these distortions, you must look at the results of the behaviors. What kind of physical toll have these cognitive distortions had on your body and in your relationships? Challenging these distortions with your humanity (being human with a wide range of emotions and physical limitations) and with facts will force you to rethink your responsibilities and task list. It will also make you re-evaluate the pressure to perform.

What are the "facts" in your life? Ask yourself, if I stop, will it continue? If I rest, will it go on? If I take a break, will it fall apart? If the answer is yes to these questions, then you may have created a system that totally depends on you, or you don't trust those working with and around you. The fact is that your cognitive distortion or flawed view of your own abilities have caused you to create systems that operate totally around you. The facts are supposed to challenge the faulty thinking, not reinforce them. In order to drop your cape, you're going to have to challenge these distortions and rebuild your systems based on everyone's ability, not just yours.

Reflection Questions

Think of some of your superwoman thoughts and behaviors.

- What can you list as cognitive distortion?
- What thoughts feed the need for you to continue wearing the cape?
- How can you redirect those thoughts so that the outcome has a collaborative result and all the pressure isn't on you?

Trust Issues

It is common for people to internalize disappointments, deficiencies and abandonment. These experiences may result in the "*I just got to get it done... Put on your big girl panties.... Somebody's gotta do it... No one else will do it, so I will.*" These frames of thought, while sometimes necessary, cause us to rely only on ourselves and be less trusting of others.

Before I began taking off my cape, I would plan events and programs alone. At times, I wouldn't want help because by the time I would explain what to do, I could have done it. Other times there was no one there to help. This was probably because of my bad attitude caused by my heightened anxiety, which stopped people from offering their help.

Thinking you are better off alone and doing things by yourself causes a tremendous amount of stress when most times there are people willing to help you. Besides, is faster always better anyway? I get it, completing tasks and meeting deadlines are important. But sometimes wearing the cape can make you appear selfish, untrusting of your team members and an attention hog.

Lack of trust has to be challenged. Much like the defense mechanisms and cognitive distortions mentioned before, you have to challenge your lack of trust by your results and by the facts. Is it working for you? Are you creating meaningful relationships? Are you creating a system that isn't based on your presence, therefore allowing more time for you? I'm not suggesting you trust everyone, but I do suggest using discretion and trusting others more when appropriate.

Reflection Questions

- Is it hard for you to trust others?
- If so, where does this lack of trust come from.
- Is this something you are currently working on?
- How has lack of trust influenced your career, friendships and relationships?

Strength vs. Weakness

You are strong and beautiful, but your strength does not take away from your human nature (having a wide range of emotions and physical limitations). True strength is found in a woman who takes care of herself. We have to teach the generation coming after us to take care of themselves. Gone are the days where we are empty by the end of the day and have nothing else to give. If you are in a time in your life when you are building, there will be times when you have to work late, and burn the midnight oil, but that should not be a way of life. There are appropriate times to put on the cape; times when you need a "just get it done" mindset in order to complete a task: however, there will be plenty more times when you need to remove the cape.

As Superwoman, you want/need to be there for others, helping them and showing your strength. But everyone has a time in their life when they have to stop leaning on others and prove to themselves that they are strong as well. We have to show our strength by allowing others to show theirs. **Strength is not always measured by what you can carry or hold on to. It's also measured by what you let go.**

Asking for help does not make you weak! Weakness is the state or condition of lacking strength. Strength is the quality or state of being physically strong or the capacity of an object or substance to withstand great force or pressure. As Superwomen, we are taught, groomed and expected to withstand force, pressure and the weight of the world on our shoulders. When life comes against us hard, we fight with all we have. We sacrifice ourselves in order to ensure the safety of our loved ones, our jobs and our image. Again, I understand and validate that this is necessary and non-negotiable at times. *However, we also have to make sure that we are not carrying a burden, lesson, or experience that belongs to someone else.*

Sitting in your car to gather your strength and thoughts at the end of a long day, falling asleep at your desk, going without eating or binging on unhealthy snacks because you can't catch a break are not signs of strength or a badge of honor. There is a distinct difference between having a strong work ethic and being overworked, and your body will make the distinction. Fatigue, headaches, insomnia, lack of motivation, etc. may all be signs of burnout. Burnout is not a sign of weakness, but a reminder of your humanity.

You were created to be a great figure in this world, but contrary to what you were taught, you are not immortal. You are not a superhuman, metahuman or mutant. **You are a human.** You were made with penetrable skin, breakable bones and fragile emotions. No matter how tough our protective armor is, we are still human and deserve to be treated as such by ourselves and others. This does not mean we can't relish in our powers at times, but we have to know when to remove the armor and allow ourselves to be vulnerable. Vulnerability - what seems like a curse word at times - is usually the state in which we heal. Being vulnerable and allowing ourselves to be open and honest, provides the opportunity to shred weight, burdens and fears while receiving love, grace and understanding. So make no mistake about it: **there is no weakness in your humanity.** There is strength, grace and vulnerability.

Reflection Questions

- How do you define your strength?
- How has your definition of strength impacted or influenced your behavior?
- Is it hard for you to ask for help?
- How do you define weakness?
- Do you believe that showing humanity and vulnerability is a sign of weakness?

Pressure to Perform

In a professional setting, it's not uncommon to feel as if you have to perform. If you are both female and a person of color, you may feel twice the pressure of your colleagues. Pressure to be better, funnier, a team player, not too aggressive, not too much of a pushover, the listener and the mediator all while getting work done is breaking the backs of professional women of color across the globe.

Microaggressions, lack of communication and downright disrespect aren't enough to stop you, but they put you in a constant state of stress and that can be harmful to the body over time. Requiring respect in the professional setting seems to be a fine line to walk because of patriarchy and expectations. Nevertheless, it's important that we change the narrative in professional settings by accepting nothing less than being respected, heard and treated fairly.

1. **Stop doing everyone's job.** It is not our responsibility to pick up the slack of our co-workers or even our boss. Stop breaking your back for a company that would replace you without a second thought.

2. **Use your benefits.** Your colleagues will call out, take vacation or sick leave whenever they need or want. You don't get a gold star for perfect attendance if you burn out. Poor self-care is only going to lead you to a hospital stay or doctor's note requiring time off.

3. **You don't have to play therapist, comedian or any other role not in your job description.** Being "on" all the time is exhausting and if you just want to hunker down and work without the extra crap, do you, sis!

4. **Demand respect in a professional way.** If you were slacking in any way, you better believe everyone in leadership would be cc'd on an email throwing you under the bus. So, if you are being treated in any way other than with professional courtesy, then you need to make it known. You can't do your job without respect and communication. You may perform miracles on your job, but with professionalism, teamwork and mutual respect, you may not have to. You may find that being respected and treated equally allows others to pick up slack and relieves you of the additional stress.

Reflection Questions

- Do you feel pressure to perform in your family or career?
- Do you feel pressured to uphold an image?
- Do you feel an underlining pressure to dispel a stigma or stereotype, therefore working harder than your peers for little to no recognition from your superiors?
- What steps can be taken to relieve this pressure?

Poor Boundaries

It's common to feel guilty when someone really needs or wants something from you, but you just don't want to, don't have the energy or money to do it. If you're wearing the cape, you'll do it anyway or find a way to get it done. While others may see this as an accomplishment, I see it as poor boundaries. Any time you feel guilty, pressured or persuaded into something that you don't want to do, you are being manipulated, taken advantage of and you are disregarding your own boundaries. I'm not saying everything is manipulation, but if you have to be convinced, pressured or persuaded because you already have so much on your plate, then your boundaries need to be tightened up.

Why do you think people always call you? Yes, you are good at what you do, but could it also be that they know you will give in? Does sharing their sob story, telling you all that they have going on and expressing how much they need you, force you to say yes? They know you will give in even if it means disregarding your own feelings, fatigue and unrelenting schedule.

Practice saying no to help you establish boundaries. Being supportive does not mean you must neglect yourself. In fact, if you continue to disregard personal and professional boundaries, you won't be any good to anyone due to the pending burnout.

Reflection Questions

- Do you say yes, even when you want to say no?
- Are you uncomfortable using the word no, even when it will benefit you in the long run?
- Do you ignore your internal warning signs?
- How can you improve your boundaries?

Teaching vs. Enabling

You can do it faster. It's easier to just do it yourself. You already know where everything is to get it done. While all of these statements are true, what are the people around you learning in the process? If you like your place cleaned a certain way but never teach, correct, or redirect those in your household, then how do you expect them to learn? Doing it yourself all the time will lead to burnout, resentment and frustration. Doing it all yourself also prevents others from learning, growing and supporting you in the process. While the teaching process may cost you some time and sanity, there comes a point when teaching will save your sanity later on.

Enabling usually comes after years of not teaching, redirecting or empowering with knowledge. I view this as a result of always doing things yourself and not teaching the valuable lessons necessary for independence and life to take place at the appropriate developmental stages. For example, when I was a resident assistant in college, we usually started the school year off with welcome banners and boards. Posted on those boards were

31

step by step instructions on how to wash and dry clothes. Incoming freshmen majoring in biology, psychology and education with exceptional SAT scores had no clue of how to wash the funk from their clothes. This is an example of enabling; whether or not it was required in their home, it still wasn't a conversation before they moved into their dorm.

While you are great at what you do, teaching others instead of enabling will free you from some of the responsibility.

Overfunctioning and underfunctioning are terms that can also describe enabling behaviors. When you overfunction, you allow others around you to underfunction. In order for any relationship to operate appropriately there needs to be equal functioning. Of course there are times when you may need to do more or less but this should never be a permanent way of operating. Overfunctioning happens easily and subconsciously. It's usually brought to your attention once you become frustrated with the pattern. For example, let's say early in your relationship you cook and clean the kitchen daily. At first it's "fine" maybe even "fun". Then after a few months you realize that your spouse never offers to help. This starts to irritate you, but you don't say anything, you just wait to see how long it takes for your spouse to offer. Months later, you explode with anger and hurt because now you feel your spouse is inconsiderate and taking you for granted. Your spouse, however, is totally lost and confused because he thought you "liked to do it." This is not only a prime example of overfunctioning but also a great example of unspoken expectations. In the beginning, you did the cooking and cleaning without request. While offered help is nice, you are responsible for communicating your needs and can request help early on. This prevents all future resentments, frustration and blow-ups because the shared expectations are discussed. No overfunctioning and no underfunctioning.

Overfunctioning also robs the opportunity of growth. If you overfunction this takes away your counterpart's ability to change. If you always do it, when can they ? How can they?

Reflection Questions

- Can your recall a moment when you enabled someone?
- How are you still being impacted by past enabling behaviors?
- What needs to change within you to release the enabling/overfunctioning patterns.
- How will your life improve when you stop enabling/overfunctioning?

Dropping The Cape

We've discussed why we need to drop the cape, but let's get into how.

1. **Make the decision to put yourself first instead of last.** As women, it is our nature to nurture and care for others. But that does not have to always come at the expense of caring for ourselves. Make the decision to care for your mind, body and spirit.

2. **Discover who you are in the current phase of your life.** Over the past 10 years, I have learned so much about myself. What I've learned is that as a human being who's constantly learning and embarking on new adventures, I am an ever-changing person. By high school, I learned to love myself, and I really knew who I was. In college, I grew, learned and evolved, and I continued to love myself, but I changed again over the next decade through marriage, tragedy and then motherhood. I learned more and more about myself in each stage. Sometimes I was pleased, and sometimes I was not, thus prompting major work and change to take place. In every phase of life, I had to become acquainted with

the evolving person and make sure her needs were being met and that she was doing her part to meet the needs of those she was responsible for. What worked back then, may not work so well now. Keep discovering yourself.

3. **Change your thoughts.** *Start With Your Thoughts: A Workbook To Improve Self-Esteem and Eliminate Negative Thinking* is a workbook I created to help change the way we think. This workbook pairs well with improving the negative thought patterns and cognitive distortions associated with wearing the cape or the Superwoman Syndrome. When you change your thinking, you change your behavior. The workbook can be purchased online at kiaratmoore.com/resources

4. **Act.** After you figure out what you need in this phase of your life, make a plan of action. I know self-care and wellness have become cliche, but they really are keys to a healthy life. Take care of yourself first! When you treat your body well, it functions properly and you will live to enjoy your family. When you manage your emotional and mental health appropriately (communicating thoughts, needs, desires, going to therapy, not holding in resentment or anger) you are able to have positive interactions and create meaningful

connections. It all works out for your benefit and for those directly connected to you.

5. **Release.** Release the notion that you have to do it all. One thing that I will never forget is how expendable I was at a job that I thought I did very well. I made great connections and made the company look great, yet I was let go without thought when budget cuts were made. I realised that life goes on without you. People will continue to live with or without you. Although you make a difference or impact in their life, without you, it will still go on. But if you sacrifice all of your life for others, then when do you get to live? You don't. You can't get anything back from the past, but you can ensure that you live every remaining day with purpose, joy and peace.

6. **Communicate.** Everyone doesn't change just because you decided to change. Actually, deciding to change may stir the pot with those around you. People often become comfortable with routines, especially when they benefit from the routine. Your decision to change is going to change their routine and comfort level. Expect some push back, but don't be dismayed or discouraged. Be consistent. Your new consistent pattern of doing less and requiring more will eventually be accepted, unless they are only interested in taking advantage of you. Then, you may lose some

people. Either way, it is important to communicate with those close to you that you are making positive changes in your life and it will mean changes in how you engage with them. When they call you "brand new," embrace it and reply, "Yes! This is a brand new me!"

7. **Rehearse.** Change requires repetition. It is not always miraculous and immediate. It's hard, uncomfortable and confusing at times. For Superwoman, it can also cause you to feel guilty. Nevertheless, keep going. Remember I'm not suggesting that you cut everyone off and "Do you!" No, I'm simply reminding you that you don't have to do it all. You deserve to put yourself first and live your life embracing your humanity. Keep practicing! The rewards will be assuring and you will feel empowered. Using sick days when you need them, taking vacations, saying no, saying yes when it fits in your schedule, removing internalized obligation and implementing self-care will have major pay offs and result in a boost of self-esteem and joy.

8. **Make a wellness plan and stick to it!** See next chapter.

8 Areas of Wellness

I reference the eight areas of wellness to offer a holistic approach to wellness. By focusing on and improving each of these 8 areas, you will feel fulfilled and your quality of life will improve. When you're wearing your cape, you usually neglect yourself in one or more of the following areas.

Emotional Wellness—Coping effectively with life and creating satisfying relationships. There are many ways to achieve emotional wellness. Seeking counseling for unresolved pain, trauma or for emotional balance, reading books, completing self-help journals, and daily practice are just a few examples.

In order for the Superwoman reading this guide to achieve emotional wellness, each concern previously mentioned must be addressed and challenged on a daily basis. Emotional wellness, like everything else, is a goal that must be practiced and followed through. Much like changing your diet, changing your thought and behavior patterns requires will power, consistency and intentionality. Because of the nature of this challenge, I suggest seeking help from a mental health professional while using this guide to support you and help you work out your attachment to your cape. In order to achieve emotional wellness, your thought processes, behavior patterns, priorities and relationships must be evaluated and adjusted.

Spiritual Wellness—*Expanding a sense of purpose and meaning in life. Seeking understanding through personal study and experience with your creator/source of hope.*

For the Christian Superwoman, I want to dispel a major myth. YOU ARE NOT JESUS; YOU CAN'T SAVE THE WORLD. For some reason, some Christians believe that they have to give everything and be martyrs. Give to the poor? Feed the hungry? Clothe the naked? Be a good witness by sharing the gospel? Yes, yes, yes, and oh yes! But where does it say that you have to die and rise again in 3 days? Where does it say you are the savior of the world? Oh, it doesn't? Could that be because that's already been done? Even Jesus rested. Let's take a note from Him and do the same.

We have to realize that we can't save the world and that our participation, good deeds and seeds planted are enough. This allows others to have time and space to grow and mature in their spiritual walk as well. If God is trying to work on someone's heart, but you keep intervening, you are going to do more hurt than harm by not giving them space to grow for themselves.

Social Wellness—*Developing a sense of connection, belonging, and a well-developed support system. With a balanced level of self-reflection and trust in deserving companions, you can build a great network of reciprocating friends.*

Having great friends is a wonderful feeling. But with the cape, friendship is complicated. Although Superwoman has a great time with her friends, she probably still feels lonely and isolated at times. She probably is the go to for all their problems and probably is the event planner for the group. On the other hand, she may seldomly make time to enjoy her friends because she is too busy enabling others and trying to save the world.

Connections and belonging are basic human needs. By dropping your cape and focusing on your human abilities, thoughts and feelings, you will have true connections by showing your vulnerabilities and your true self.

Physical Wellness—*Recognizing the need for physical activity, healthy foods, and sleep. The level of functioning in your physical body is crucial to the connections between your mind, spirit, and body. Your physical functioning also impacts how well you can manage any other area of wellness and must be* *in your top three priorities. How you manage your physical body may vary (diet, exercise, etc..), but taking care of yourself physically cannot be an afterthought.*

Mind, body and spirit - this is how you were created. This is the makeup of your humanity. It is imperative to care for and treat all three properly and appropriately. When one is mistreated or malnourished, all three will systematically and simultaneously shut down. The cross over and connection is astonishing, so if you want to improve one, you must improve all three. Your body is a temple, and you only get one. Treat it with the respect it deserves by feeding it properly, hydrating it and exercising it. Most importantly, give your body rest. Most of the body's healing takes place in your sleep. Allow your body to operate at full capacity by improving the time, attention and maintenance you provide.

Intellectual Wellness—*Recognizing creative abilities and finding ways to expand knowledge and skills. Knowledge is power. Increase your power by learning more about your career field, interests and hobbies.*

While wearing the cape, we tend to know a lot - at least we think we do - because we are able to think fast on our feet to solve a problem. Usually solving that problem just means we find a way to do it ourselves. Wouldn't it be great if we channeled this ability to adapt into something productive and in an area of growth for our personal lives, careers and futures? What if, instead of pushing everyone else ahead, we followed our dream, and increased our knowledge in areas that benefit or bring pleasure to our lives? Learn something, try something new, and stretch your perspectives in order to open yourself up the world of possibilities you live in.

Occupational Wellness—*Personal satisfaction and enrichment from one's work. If you hate your job, there are ways out. Search within yourself for your true passions and pursue them. So, what if you have to stay at the job you hate until you reach your goal? You are never wasting time if you are making strides in the right direction. Don't despise your small beginnings. To become an oak tree, you have to endure the lifespan of the acorn.*

Most people spend the majority of their day at work or working. A normal shift is one-third of your day, so I would strongly suggest finding a career that you don't just enjoy but that you are passionate about. Much like the need to tie on the cape at times, there are times when we are working to pay the bills, gain experience, or as I like to say, fund the dream. Also like the cape, there comes a time to drop the cape, and drop the filler jobs and go after what makes you work with a smile on your face or at least feel fulfilled at the end of the day.

Financial Wellness—Satisfaction with current and future financial situations. Financial wellness is not only about what's coming in but also what's going out. Financial wellness may include learning to make responsible and healthy financial choices.

Superwoman usually stretches herself thin in many areas, and the area of finance isn't much different. Some people give all they have, others spend all they have. Where do you fall in this spectrum? Financial freedom is as important to one's mental health and overall life as any other area of wellness. If you have a problem with too much charitable giving or too much anxious, depressed or reparative shopping (also known as retail therapy) it is imperative that you manage your finances more appropriately. Money doesn't buy you happiness, but not being in good financial standing will negatively affect your mood and impact your outlook.

Environmental Wellness—Good health by occupying pleasant, stimulating environments that support well-being. Your environment has the power to directly impact your mood and productivity. If you are an adult, you have ultimate control over your environment. It may take time and effort to create the environment that works best for you, but it will be worth it.

There is so much talk about the decline of our world. Pollution, poor air and water quality and global warming are causing major and damaging effects. If poor environmental control can impact our entire planet, how do you think poor environmental control will impact your surroundings? Hopefully, you wouldn't allow trash and debri to infest your physical home, and your emotional and mental environments should have the same standards. One of the best feelings of being an adult with your own resources is that you don't have to stay anywhere you don't feel comfortable. Leaving a party or hostile environment is liberating once you realize you have control over yourself. When you operate in this control, you can manage who you allow into your personal space. Hopefully, you allow some people who will lift you up and encourage you, not because you are wearing the cape, but because you are a wonderful woman deserving of the same love, support and kindness that you give.

By now, I hope that you've at least loosened if not thrown you cape down. I know it will take time, practice and patience. Many of our capes are like the cape on Marvel's *Dr. Strange* where the cape flies and attaches itself on its own, so it will take some time to drop it for good. However, the awareness that your cape exists is a powerful first step. Implementing what you learned in this book will take you through a wonderful journey of change, self-care and self-compassion.

DROP THE CAPE! Live a life of SELF-CARE, WELLNESS AND REAL STRENGTH!

Use the following scale to assess your feelings as you work towards self-care, wellness and strength. On a scale of 1 to 10, with 1 being not at all and 10 being very much, rate how you feel right now in the following categories:

Satisfied with your current life
1 2 3 4 5 6 7 8 9 10

Fulfilled in your career
1 2 3 4 5 6 7 8 9 10

Satisfied with your current level of self-care
1 2 3 4 5 6 7 8 9 10

Fulfilled in your relationships
1 2 3 4 5 6 7 8 9 10

Feeling overwhelmed
1 2 3 4 5 6 7 8 9 10

Feeling anxious
1 2 3 4 5 6 7 8 9 10

Feeling restless
1 2 3 4 5 6 7 8 9 10

Feeling underappreciated or undervalued
1 2 3 4 5 6 7 8 9 10

In need of a break/vacation
1 2 3 4 5 6 7 8 9 10

In need of professional/personal boundaries
1 2 3 4 5 6 7 8 9 10

About the Author

Kiara Moore is a Licensed Professional Counselor for Mental Health (LPCMH) in the state of Delaware. Kiara enjoys working with adolescents and adults. Kiara takes an eclectic approach and utilizes several evidence based treatment approaches focused on the needs of the individual, couple or family.

Kiara Moore, LPCMH is also a public speaker and author of five books:

- *When I'm Angry*
- *The Pursuit of Productivity Planner*
- *Start With Your Thoughts: A Workbook To Improve Self-Esteem and Eliminate Negative Thinking*
- *Start With Your Thoughts: A Workbook To Improve Self-Esteem and Eliminate Negative Thinking (Teen Version)*
- *Drop Your Cape: A Guide To Increase Self-Care, Wellness and Strength.*

All books are available on Amazon and through her website kiaratmoore.com.

Connect with and book Kiara Moore, LPCMH
Kiaratmoore.com
kmtherapeuticservices@gmail.com

Facebook and Instagram
@kiaramooretherapeuticservices

Made in the USA
Columbia, SC
10 November 2021

48703693R20033